TWO GREAT ONES BY
ALBEE

In *THE SANDBOX* an old woman prepares to die, while daughter, son-in-law, and the Angel of Death keep watch. "The piece began where so many impudent collages have begun, and then went on to insinuate, at no more than a whisper, a mood that embraced all of the diverse elements and turned them into a single, oddly satisfying sigh."—*Walter Kerr*, N.Y. Herald Tribune

THE DEATH OF BESSIE SMITH is a powerful drama that bares the ugly and shameful circumstances surrounding the tragic death of a great Negro blues singer. ". . . while the incident, itself, was brawling at me, and while the characters I had elected to carry the tale were wrestling it from me, I discovered I was, in fact, writing about something at the same time slightly removed from and more pertinent to what I had imagined. . . . I know only that the play, printed here, is, whatever its failings or successes may be, most exactly what I had to say on the matter."
—*Edward Albee*

Other SIGNET Plays

The Sandbox
The Death of Bessie Smith

(WITH Fam and Yam)

BY EDWARD ALBEE

A SIGNET BOOK PUBLISHED BY
THE NEW AMERICAN LIBRARY

CONTENTS

The Sandbox (1959)

A BRIEF PLAY, IN MEMORY OF MY GRANDMOTHER (1876-1959)

Music by William Flanagan

FIRST PERFORMANCE: April 15, 1960. New York City.

The Jazz Gallery.

The Sandbox

The Players:

THE YOUNG MAN	.... 25.	A good-looking, well-built boy in a bathing suit.
MOMMY	.... 55.	A well-dressed, imposing woman.
DADDY	.... 60.	A small man; gray, thin.
GRANDMA	.... 86.	A tiny, wizened woman with bright eyes.
THE MUSICIAN	......	No particular age, but young would be nice.

Note:

When, in the course of the play, MOMMY and DADDY call each other by these names, there should be no suggestion of regionalism. These names are of empty affection and point up the pre-senility and vacuity of their characters.

The Scene:

A bare stage, with only the following: Near the footlights, far stage-right, two simple chairs set side by side, facing the audience; near the footlights, far stage-left, a chair facing stage-right with a music stand before it; farther back, and stage-center, slightly elevated and raked, a large child's sandbox with a toy pail and shovel; the background is the sky, which alters from brightest day to deepest night.

At the beginning, it is brightest day; the YOUNG
MAN is alone on stage, to the rear of the sandbox,
and to one side. He is doing calesthenics; he does
calesthenics until quite at the very end of the play.
These calesthenics, employing the arms only,
should suggest the beating and fluttering of wings.
The YOUNG MAN is, after all, the Angel of Death.

MOMMY *and* DADDY *enter from stage-left,* MOMMY
first.

MOMMY
(*Motioning to* DADDY) Well, here we are; this is the
beach.

DADDY (*Whining*)
I'm cold.

MOMMY
(*Dismissing him with a little laugh*) Don't be silly; it's as
warm as toast. Look at that nice young man over there:
he doesn't think it's cold. (*Waves to the* YOUNG MAN)
Hello.

YOUNG MAN
(*With an endearing smile*) Hi!

MOMMY (*Looking about*)
This will do perfectly . . . don't you think so, Daddy?
There's sand there . . . and the water beyond. What do
you think, Daddy?

DADDY *(Vaguely)*

Whatever you say, Mommy.

MOMMY

(With the same little laugh) Well, of course . . . whatever I say. Then, it's settled, is it?

DADDY *(Shrugs)*

She's *your* mother, not mine.

MOMMY

I know she's my mother. What do you take me for? (*A pause*) All right, now; let's get on with it. (*She shouts into the wings, stage-left*) You! Out there! You can come in now.

> (*The* MUSICIAN *enters, seats himself in the chair, stage-left, places music on the music stand, is ready to play.* MOMMY *nods approvingly*)

MOMMY

Very nice; very nice. Are you ready, Daddy? Let's go get Grandma.

DADDY

Whatever you say, Mommy.

MOMMY

(*Leading the way out, stage-left*) Of course, whatever I say. (*To the* MUSICIAN) You can begin now.

> (*The* MUSICIAN *begins playing;* MOMMY *and* DADDY *exit; the* MUSICIAN, *all the while playing, nods to the* YOUNG MAN)

YOUNG MAN

(*With the same endearing smile*) Hi!

> (*After a moment,* MOMMY *and* DADDY *re-enter, carrying* GRANDMA. *She is borne in by their hands*

*under her armpits; she is quite rigid; her legs are
drawn up; her feet do not touch the ground; the
expression on her ancient face is that of puzzle-
ment and fear)*

DADDY

Where do we put her?

MOMMY

(The same little laugh) Wherever I say, of course. Let
me see . . . well . . . all right, over there . . . in the
sandbox. *(Pause)* Well, what are you waiting for,
Daddy? . . . The sandbox!

> *(Together they carry* GRANDMA *over to the sand-
> box and more or less dump her in)*

GRANDMA

*(Righting herself to a sitting position; her voice a cross
between a baby's laugh and cry)* Ahhhhhh! Graaaaa!

DADDY *(Dusting himself)*

What do we do now?

MOMMY

(To the MUSICIAN*)* You can stop now.
> *(The* MUSICIAN *stops)*
(Back to DADDY*)* What do you mean, what do we do
now? We go over there and sit down, of course. *(To the*
YOUNG MAN*)* Hello there.

YOUNG MAN

(Again smiling) Hi!

> *(*MOMMY *and* DADDY *move to the chairs, stage-
> right, and sit down. A pause)*

GRANDMA

(*Same as before*) Ahhhhhh! Ah-haaaaaa! Graaaaaa!

DADDY

Do you think . . . do you think she's . . . comfortable?

MOMMY (*Impatiently*)

How would I know?

DADDY

(*Pause*) What do we do now?

MOMMY

(*As if remembering*) We . . . wait. We . . . sit here . . . and we wait . . . that's what we do.

DADDY

(*After a pause*) Shall we talk to each other?

MOMMY

(*With that little laugh; picking something off her dress*) Well, *you* can talk, if you want to . . . if you can think of anything to *say* . . . if you can think of anything *new*.

DADDY (*Thinks*)

No . . . I suppose not.

MOMMY

(*With a triumphant laugh*) Of course not!

GRANDMA

(*Banging the toy shovel against the pail*) Haaaaaa! Ah-haaaaaa!

MOMMY

(*Out over the audience*) Be quiet, Grandma . . . just be quiet, and wait.

(GRANDMA *throws a shovelful of sand at* MOMMY)

MOMMY

(*Still out over the audience*) She's throwing sand at me! You stop that, Grandma; you stop throwing sand at Mommy! (*To* DADDY) She's throwing sand at me.

(DADDY *looks around at* GRANDMA, *who screams at him*)

GRANDMA

GRAAAAA!

MOMMY

Don't look at her. Just . . . sit here . . . be very still . . . and wait. (*To the* MUSICIAN) You . . . uh . . . you go ahead and do whatever it is you do.

(*The* MUSICIAN *plays*)

(MOMMY *and* DADDY *are fixed, staring out beyond the audience.* GRANDMA *looks at them, looks at the* MUSICIAN, *looks at the sandbox, throws down the shovel*)

GRANDMA

Ah-haaaaaa! Graaaaaa! (*Looks for reaction; gets none. Now . . . directly to the audience*) Honestly! What a way to treat an old woman! Drag her out of the house . . . stick her in a car . . . bring her out here from the city . . . dump her in a pile of sand . . . and leave her here to set. I'm eighty-six years old! I was married when I was seventeen. To a farmer. He died when I was thirty. (*To the* MUSICIAN) Will you stop that, please?

(*The* MUSICIAN *stops playing*)

I'm a feeble old woman . . . how do you expect anybody

to hear me over that peep! peep! peep! (*To herself*)
There's no respect around here. (*To the* YOUNG MAN)
There's no respect around here!

YOUNG MAN

(*Same smile*) Hi!

GRANDMA

(*After a pause, a mild double-take, continues, to the
audience*) My husband died when I was thirty (*indicates*
MOMMY), and I had to raise that big cow over there all
by my lonesome. You can imagine what *that was like*.
Lordy! (*To the* YOUNG MAN) Where'd they get *you*?

YOUNG MAN

Oh . . . I've been around for a while.

GRANDMA

I'll bet you have! Heh, heh, heh. Will you look at you!

YOUNG MAN

(*Flexing his muscles*) Isn't that something? (*Continues
his calesthenics*)

GRANDMA

Boy, oh boy; I'll say. Pretty good.

YOUNG MAN (*Sweetly*)

I'll say.

GRANDMA

Where ya from?

YOUNG MAN

Southern California.

GRANDMA *(Nodding)*

Figgers; figgers. What's your name, honey?

YOUNG MAN

I don't know. . . .

GRANDMA

(To the audience) Bright, too!

YOUNG MAN

I mean . . . I mean, they haven't given me one yet . . . the studio . . .

GRANDMA

(Giving him the once-over) You don't say . . . you don't say. Well . . . uh, I've got to talk some more . . . don't you go 'way.

YOUNG MAN

Oh, no.

GRANDMA

(Turning her attention back to the audience) Fine; fine. *(Then, once more, back to the* YOUNG MAN*)* You're . . . you're an actor, hunh?

YOUNG MAN *(Beaming)*

Yes. I am.

GRANDMA

(To the audience again; shrugs) I'm smart that way. *Anyhow,* I had to raise . . . *that* over there all by my lonesome; and what's next to her there . . . that's what she married. Rich? I tell you . . . money, money, money. They took me off the *farm* . . . which was real decent of them . . . and they moved me into the big town house with *them* . . . fixed a nice place for me under the stove

. . . gave me an army blanket . . . and my own dish . . . my very own dish! So, what have I got to complain about? Nothing, of course. I'm not complaining. (*She looks up at the sky, shouts to someone off stage*) Shouldn't it be getting dark now, dear?

> (*The lights dim; night comes on. The* MUSICIAN *begins to play; it becomes deepest night. There are spots on all the players, including the* YOUNG MAN, *who is, of course, continuing his calisthenics*)

DADDY (*Stirring*)

It's nighttime.

MOMMY

Shhhh. Be still . . . wait.

DADDY (*Whining*)

It's so hot.

MOMMY

Shhhhhh. Be still . . . wait.

GRANDMA

(*To herself*) That's better. Night. (*To the* MUSICIAN) Honey, do you play all through this part?
> (*The* MUSICIAN *nods*)

Well, keep it nice and soft; that's a good boy.
> (*The* MUSICIAN *nods again; plays softly*)

That's nice.
> (*There is an off-stage rumble*)

DADDY (*Starting*)

What was that?

MOMMY

(*Beginning to weep*) It was nothing.

DADDY

It was . . . it was . . . thunder . . . or a wave breaking
. . . or something.

MOMMY

(*Whispering, through her tears*) It was an off-stage rumble . . . and you know what *that* means. . . .

DADDY

I forget. . . .

MOMMY

(*Barely able to talk*) It means the time has come for
poor Grandma . . . and I can't bear it!

DADDY (*Vacantly*)

I . . . I suppose you've got to be brave.

GRANDMA (*Mocking*)

That's right, kid; be brave. You'll bear up; you'll get over
it.
  (*Another off-stage rumble . . . louder*)

MOMMY

Ohhhhhhhhhh . . . poor Grandma . . . poor Grandma. . . .

GRANDMA (*To* MOMMY)

I'm fine! I'm all right! It hasn't happened yet!
  (*A violent off-stage rumble. All the lights go out,
  save the spot on the* YOUNG MAN; *the* MUSICIAN
  stops playing)

MOMMY

Ohhhhhhhhhh. . . . Ohhhhhhhhhh. . . .

  (*Silence*)

GRANDMA

Don't put the lights up yet . . . I'm not ready; I'm not quite ready. (*Silence*) All right, dear . . . I'm about done.

> (*The lights come up again, to brightest day; the* MUSICIAN *begins to play.* GRANDMA *is discovered, still in the sandbox, lying on her side, propped up on an elbow, half covered, busily shoveling sand over herself*)

GRANDMA (*Muttering*)

I don't know how I'm supposed to do anything with this goddam toy shovel. . . .

DADDY

Mommy! It's daylight!

MOMMY (*Brightly*)

So it is! Well! Our long night is over. We must put away our tears, take off our mourning . . . and face the future. It's our duty.

GRANDMA

(*Still shoveling; mimicking*) . . . take off our mourning . . . face the future. . . . Lordy!

> (MOMMY *and* DADDY *rise, stretch.* MOMMY *waves to the* YOUNG MAN)

YOUNG MAN

(*With that smile*) Hi!

> (GRANDMA *plays dead.* (!) MOMMY *and* DADDY *go over to look at her; she is a little more than half buried in the sand; the toy shovel is in her hands, which are crossed on her breast*)

MOMMY

(*Before the sandbox; shaking her head*) Lovely! It's . . . it's hard to be sad . . . she looks . . . so happy. (*With*

pride and conviction) It pays to do things well. (*To the*
MUSICIAN) All right, you can stop now, if you want to.
I mean, stay around for a swim, or something; it's all
right with us. (*She sighs heavily*) Well, Daddy . . . off
we go.

DADDY

Brave Mommy!

MOMMY

Brave Daddy!
 (*They exit, stage-left*)

GRANDMA

(*After they leave; lying quite still*) It pays to do things
well. . . . Boy, oh boy! (*She tries to sit up*) . . . well,
kids . . . (*but she finds she can't*) . . . I . . . I can't get
up. I . . . I can't move. . . .
 (*The* YOUNG MAN *stops his calisthenics, nods to*
 the MUSICIAN, *walks over to* GRANDMA, *kneels*
 down by the sandbox)

GRANDMA

I . . . can't move. . . .

YOUNG MAN

Shhhhh . . . be very still. . . .

GRANDMA

I . . . I can't move. . . .

YOUNG MAN

Uh . . . ma'am; I . . . I have a line here.

GRANDMA

Oh, I'm sorry, sweetie; you go right ahead.

YOUNG MAN

I am . . . uh . . .

GRANDMA

Take your time, dear.

YOUNG MAN

(*Prepares; delivers the line like a real amateur*) I am the
Angel of Death. I am . . . uh . . . I am come for you.

GRANDMA

What . . . wha . . . (*Then, with resignation*) . . . ohhhh
. . . ohhhh, I see.
        (*The* YOUNG MAN *bends over, kisses* GRANDMA
        gently on the forehead)

GRANDMA

        (*Her eyes closed, her hands folded on her breast
        again, the shovel between her hands, a sweet smile
        on her face*)
Well . . . that was very nice, dear. . . .

YOUNG MAN

(*Still kneeling*) Shhhhhh . . . be still. . . .

GRANDMA

What I meant was . . . you did that very well, dear. . . .

YOUNG MAN (*Blushing*)

. . . oh . . .

GRANDMA

No; I mean it. You've got that . . . you've got a quality.

YOUNG MAN

(*With his endearing smile*) Oh . . . thank you; thank you
very much . . . ma'am.

GRANDMA

(*Slowly; softly—as the* YOUNG MAN *puts his hands on top of* GRANDMA'S) You're . . . you're welcome . . . dear.

(*Tableau. The* MUSICIAN *continues to play as the curtain slowly comes down*)

CURTAIN

The Death of Bessie Smith

A PLAY IN EIGHT SCENES (1959)

For Ned Rorem

FIRST PERFORMANCE: April 21, 1960. Berlin, Germany.

Schlosspark Theater.

The Death of Bessie Smith

The Players:

BERNIE: A Negro, about forty, thin.

JACK: A dark-skinned Negro, forty-five, bulky, with a deep voice and a mustache.

THE FATHER: A thin, balding white man, about fifty-five.

THE NURSE: A southern white girl, full blown, dark or red-haired, pretty, with a wild laugh. Twenty-six.

THE ORDERLY: A light-skinned Negro, twenty-eight, clean-shaven, trim, prim.

SECOND NURSE: A southern white girl, blond, not too pretty, about thirty.

THE INTERN: A southern white man, blond, well put-together, with an amiable face; thirty.

The Scene:

Afternoon and early evening, September 26, 1937. In and around the city of Memphis, Tennessee.

The Set:

The set for this play will vary, naturally, as stages vary—from theatre to theatre. So, the suggestions put down below, while they might serve as a useful guide, are but a general idea—what the author "sees."

What the author "sees" is this: The central and front area of the stage reserved for the admissions room of a hospital, for this is where the major portion of the action of the play takes place. The admissions desk and chair stage-center, facing the audience. A door, leading outside, stage-right; a door, leading to further areas of the hospital, stage-left. Very little more: a bench, perhaps; a chair or two. Running along the rear of the stage, and perhaps a bit on the sides, there should be a raised platform, on which, at various locations, against just the most minimal suggestions of sets, the other scenes of the play are performed. All of this very open, for the whole back wall of the stage is full of the sky, which will vary from scene to scene: a hot blue; a sunset; a great, red-orange-yellow sunset. Sometimes full, sometimes but a hint.

At the curtain, let the entire stage be dark against the sky, which is a hot blue. *Music* against this, for a moment or so, fading to under as the lights come up on:

SCENE ONE

The corner of a barroom. BERNIE *seated at a table, a beer before him, with glass.* JACK *enters, tentatively, a beer bottle in his hand; he does not see* BERNIE.

BERNIE
(*Recognizing* JACK; *with pleased surprise*) Hey!

JACK
Hm?

BERNIE
Hey; Jack!

JACK
Hm? . . . What? . . . (*Recognizes him*) Bernie!

BERNIE
What you doin' here, boy? C'mon, sit down.

JACK
Well, I'll be damned. . . .

BERNIE
C'mon, sit down, Jack.

JACK
Yeah . . . sure . . . well, I'll be damned. (*Moves over to the table; sits*) Bernie. My God, it's hot. How you been, boy?

BERNIE

Fine; fine. What you *doin'* here?

JACK

Oh, travelin'; travelin'.

BERNIE

On the move, hunh? Boy, you are the last person I expected t'walk in that door; small world, hunh?

JACK

Yeah; yeah.

BERNIE

On the move, hunh? Where you goin'?

JACK

(*Almost, but not quite, mysterious*) North.

BERNIE *(Laughs)*

North! North? That's a big place, friend: north.

JACK

Yeah . . . yeah, it is that: a big place.

BERNIE

(*After a pause; laughs again*) Well, *where,* boy? North *where?*

JACK

(*Coyly; proudly*) New York.

BERNIE

New York!

JACK

Unh-hunh; unh-hunh.

BERNIE

New York, hunh? Well. What you got goin' up there?

JACK

(*Coy again*) Oh . . . well . . . I got somethin' goin' up
there. What *you* been up to, boy?

BERNIE

New York, hunh?

JACK

(*Obviously dying to tell about it*) Unh-hunh.

BERNIE

(*Knowing it*) Well, now, isn't that somethin'. Hey! You
want a beer? You want another beer?

JACK

No, I gotta get . . . well, I don't know, I . . .

BERNIE

(*Rising from the table*) Sure you do. Hot like this? You
need a beer or two, cool you off.

JACK

(*Settling back*) Yeah; why not? Sure, Bernie.

BERNIE

(*A dollar bill in his hand; moving off*) I'll get us a pair.
New York, hunh? What's it all about, Jack? Hunh?

JACK (*Chuckles*)

Ah, you'd be surprised, boy; you'd be surprised.
    (*Lights fade on this scene, come up on another,
    which is*)

SCENE TWO

Part of a screened-in porch; some wicker furniture, a little the worse for wear.
The NURSE'S FATHER *is seated on the porch, a cane by his chair. Music, loud, from a phonograph, inside.*

FATHER

(The music is too loud; he grips the arms of his chair; finally) Stop it! Stop it! Stop it! Stop it!

NURSE *(From Inside)*

What? What did you say?

FATHER

STOP IT!

NURSE

(Appearing, dressed for duty) I can't hear you; what do you want?

FATHER

Turn it off! Turn that goddam music off!

NURSE

Honestly, Father . . .

FATHER

Turn it off!
          (The NURSE *turns wearily, goes back inside. Music stops)*
Goddamn nigger records. *(To* NURSE, *inside)* I got a headache.

NURSE   *(Re-entering)*

What?

FATHER

I said, I got a headache; you play those goddam records
all the time; blast my head off; you play those goddam
nigger records full blast . . . me with a headache. . . .

NURSE   *(Wearily)*

You take your pill?

FATHER

No!

NURSE   *(Turning)*

I'll get you your pills. . . .

FATHER

I don't want 'em!

NURSE *(Overpatiently)*

All right; then I won't get you your pills.

FATHER

(After a pause; quietly, petulantly) You play those goddam records all the time. . . .

NURSE   *(Impatiently)*

I'm sorry, Father; I didn't know you had your headache.

FATHER

Don't you use that tone with me!

NURSE

(With that tone) I wasn't using any tone. . . .

FATHER

Don't argue!

NURSE

I am not arguing; I don't *want* to argue; it's too *hot* to argue. (*Pause; then quietly*) I don't see why a person can't play a couple of records around here without . . .

FATHER

Damn noise! That's all it is; damn noise.

NURSE

(*After a pause*) I don't suppose you'll drive me to work. I don't suppose, with your headache, you feel up to driving me to the hospital.

FATHER

No.

NURSE

I didn't think you would. And I suppose *you're* going to need the car, too.

FATHER

Yes.

NURSE

Yes; I figured you would. What are you going to do, Father? Are you going to sit here all afternoon on the porch, with your headache, and *watch* the car? Are you going to sit here and watch it all afternoon? You going to sit here with a shotgun and make sure the birds don't crap on it . . . or something?

FATHER

I'm going to need it.

NURSE

Yeah; sure.

FATHER

I said, I'm going to need it.

NURSE

Yeah . . . I heard you. You're going to need it.

FATHER

I am!

NURSE

Yeah; no doubt. You going to drive down to the Democratic Club, and sit around with that bunch of loafers? You going to play big politician today? Hunh?

FATHER

That's enough, now.

NURSE

You going to go down there with that bunch of bums . . . light up one of those expensive cigars, which you have no business smoking, which you can't afford, which *I* cannot afford, to put it more accurately . . . the same brand His Honor the mayor smokes . . . you going to sit down there and talk big, about how you and the mayor are like *this* . . . you going to pretend you're something more than you really are, which is nothing but . . .

FATHER

You be quiet, you!

NURSE

. . . a hanger-on . . . a flunky . . .

FATHER

YOU BE QUIET!

NURSE *(Faster)*

Is that what you need the car for, Father, and I am going to have to take that hot, stinking bus to the hospital?

FATHER

I said, quiet! *(Pause)* I'm sick and tired of hearing you disparage my friendship with the mayor.

NURSE *(Contemptuous)*

Friendship!

FATHER

That's right: friendship.

NURSE

I'll tell you what I'll do: Now that we have His Honor, the mayor, as a patient . . . when I get down to the hospital . . . if I ever get there on that damn bus . . . I'll pay him a call, and I'll just *ask* him about your "friendship" with him; I'll just . . .

FATHER

Don't you go disturbing him; you hear me?

NURSE

Why, I should think the mayor would be de*light*ed if the daughter of one of his closest friends was to . . .

FATHER

You're going to make trouble!

NURSE *(Heavily sarcastic)*

Oh, how could I make trouble, Father?

FATHER

You be careful.

NURSE

Oh, that must be quite a friendship. Hey, I got a good idea: you could drive me down to the hospital and you could pay a visit to your good friend the mayor at the same time. Now, *that* is a good idea.

FATHER

Leave off! Just leave off!

NURSE

(Under her breath) You make me sick.

FATHER

What! What was that?

NURSE *(Very quietly)*

I said, you make me sick, Father.

FATHER

Yeah? Yeah?
> *(He takes his cane, raps it against the floor several times. This gesture, beginning in anger, alters, as it becomes weaker, to a helpless and pathetic flailing; eventually it subsides; the* NURSE *watches it all quietly)*

NURSE *(Tenderly)*

Are you done?

FATHER

Go away; go to work.

NURSE

I'll get you your pills before I go.

FATHER *(Tonelessly)*

I said, I don't want them.

NURSE

I don't care whether you *want* them, or not. . . .

FATHER

I'm not one of your patients!

NURSE

Oh, and aren't I glad you're not.

FATHER

You give them better attention than you give me!

NURSE *(Wearily)*

I don't have patients, Father; I am not a floor nurse; will you get that into your head? I am on admissions; I am on the admissions desk. You *know* that; why do you pretend otherwise?

FATHER

If you were a . . . what-do-you-call-it . . . if you were a floor nurse . . . if you *were,* you'd give your patients better attention than you give me.

NURSE

What *are* you, Father? What are you? Are you sick, or not? Are you a . . . a . . . a poor cripple, or are you planning to get yourself up out of that chair, after I go to work, and drive yourself down to the Democratic Club and sit around with that bunch of loafers? Make up your mind, Father; you can't have it every which way.

FATHER

Never mind.

NURSE

You can't; you just can't.

FATHER

Never mind, now!

NURSE

(After a pause) Well, I gotta get to work.

FATHER *(Sneering)*

Why don't you get your boy friend to drive you to work?

NURSE

All right; leave off.

FATHER

Why don't you get him to come by and pick you up, hunh?

NURSE

I said, leave off!

FATHER

Or is he only interested in driving you back here at night . . . when it's nice and dark; when it's plenty dark for messing around in his car? Is that it? Why don't you bring him here and let *me* have a look at him; why don't you let me get a look at him some time?

NURSE *(Angry)*

Well, Father . . . (*A very brief gesture at the surroundings*) maybe it's because I don't want him to get a . . .

FATHER

I hear you; I hear you at night; I hear you gigglin' and carrying on out there in his car; I hear you!

NURSE

(*Loud; to cover the sound of his voice*) I'm going, Father.

FATHER

All right; get along, then; get on!

NURSE

You're damned right!

FATHER

Go on! Go!

     (*The* NURSE *regards him for a moment; turns, exits*)

And don't stay out there all night in his car, when you get back. You hear me? (*Pause*) You hear me?

(*Lights fade on this scene; come up on*)

SCENE THREE

A bare area. JACK *enters, addresses his remarks off stage and to an invisible mirror on an invisible dresser. Music under this scene, as though coming from a distance.*

JACK

Hey . . . Bessie! C'mon, now. Hey . . . honey? Get your butt out of bed . . . wake up. C'mon; the goddam afternoon's half gone; we gotta get movin'. Hey . . . I called that son-of-a-bitch in New York . . . *I* told him, all right. I told him what you said. Wake up, baby, we gotta get out of this dump; I gotta get you to Memphis 'fore seven o'clock . . . and then . . . POW! . . . *we* are headin' straight north. Here we come; NEW YORK. I told that bastard . . . I said: Look, you don't have no exclusive rights on Bessie . . . nobody's got 'em . . . Bessie is doin' you a favor . . . she's doin' you a goddam favor. She don't *have* to sing for you. I said: Bessie's tired . . . she don't wanna travel now. An' he said: You don't *wanna* back out of this . . . Bessie told me *herself* . . . and I said: Look . . . don't worry yourself . . . Bessie said she'd cut more sides for you . . . she will . . . she'll make all the goddam new records you want. . . . What I mean to say *is*, just don't you get any ideas about havin' exclusive rights . . . because nobody's got 'em. (*Giggles*) I told him you was free as a bird, honey. Free

as a goddam bird. (*Looks in at her, shakes his head*)
Some bird! I been downstairs to check us out. I go downstairs to check us out, and I run into a friend of mine
. . . and we sit in the bar and have a few, and he says:
What're *you* doin' now; what're you doin' in this crummy
hotel? And I say: I am cartin' a bird around with me.
I'm cartin' her north; I got a fat lady upstairs; she is
sleepin' off last night. An' he says: You always got *some*
fat lady upstairs, somewhere; boy, I never seen it fail.
An' I say: This ain't just no plain fat lady I got upstairs . . . this is a celebrity, boy . . . this is a rich old
fat singin' lady . . . an' he laughed an' he said: Boy,
who you got up there? I say: You guess. An' he says:
C'mon . . . I can't *guess*. An' I told him . . . I am travelin'
with Miss Bessie Smith. An' he looked at me, an' he
said, real quiet: Jesus, boy, are you travelin' with Bessie?
An' I said . . . an' real proud: You're damn right I'm
travelin' with Bessie. An' he wants to meet you; so you
get your big self out of bed; we're goin' to go downstairs, 'cause I wanna show you off. C'mon, now; I mean
I *gotta* show you off. 'Cause then he said: "Whatever
happened to Bessie? An' I said: What do you mean,
whatever happened to Bessie? She's right upstairs. An' he
said: I mean, what's she been doin' the past four-five
years? There was a time there, boy, Chicago an' all, New
York, she was the hottest goddam thing goin'. Is she still
singin'? YOU HEAR THAT? That's what he said: Is
she still singin'? An' I said . . . I said, you been tired
. . . you been restin'. You ain't been forgotten, honey,
but they are askin' questions. SO YOU GET UP! We're
drivin' north tonight, an' when you get in New York . . .
you show 'em where you been. Honey, you're gonna go
back on top again . . . I mean it . . . you *are*. I'm gonna
get you up to New York. 'Cause you gotta make that
date. I mean, sure, baby, you're free as a goddam bird,
an' I did tell that son-of-a-bitch he don't have exclusive
rights on you . . . but, honey . . . he *is* interested . . .

an' you gotta hustle for it now. You do; 'cause if you don't do *somethin'*, people are gonna stop askin' where you been the past four-five years . . . they're gonna stop askin' anything at all! You hear? An' if I say downstairs you're rich . . . that don't make it so, Bessie. No more, honey. You gotta make this goddam trip . . . you gotta get goin' again. (*Pleading*) Baby? Honey? You know I'm not lyin' to you. C'mon now; get up. We go downstairs to the bar an' have a few . . . see my friend . . . an' then we'll get in that car . . . and *go*. 'Cause it's gettin' late, honey . . . it's gettin' awful late. (*Brighter*) Hey! You awake? (*Moving to the wings*) Well, c'mon, then, Bessie . . . let's get up. We're goin' north again!

    (*The lights fade on this scene.*
    Music.
    The sunset is predominant)

JACK'S VOICE

Ha, ha; thanks; thanks a lot. (*Car door slams. Car motor starts*) O.K.; here we go; we're on our way. (*Sound of car motor gunning, car moving off, fading*)

    (*The sunset dims again.*
    Music, fading, as the lights come up on)

SCENE FOUR

The admissions room of the hospital. The NURSE *is at her desk; the* ORDERLY *stands to one side.*

ORDERLY

The mayor of Memphis! I went into his room and there he was; the mayor of Memphis. Lying right there, flat on

his belly . . . a cigar in his mouth . . . an unlit cigar
stuck in his mouth, chewing on it, chewing on a big, unlit cigar . . . shuffling a lot of papers in his hands, a pil-
low shoved up under his chest to give him some freedom
for all those papers . . . and I came in, and I said: Good
afternoon, Your Honor . . . and he swung his face 'round
and he looked at me and he shouted: My ass hurts,
you get the hell out of here!

NURSE   *(Laughs freely)*

His Honor has got his ass in a sling, and that's for sure.

ORDERLY

And I got out; I left very quickly; I closed the door fast.

NURSE

The mayor and his hemorrhoids . . . the mayor's late
hemorrhoids . . . are a matter of deep concern to this in-
stitution, for the mayor built this hospital; the mayor is
here with his ass in a sling, and the seat of government
is now in Room 206 . . . so you be nice and respectful.
(Laughs) There is a man two rooms down who walked
in here last night after you went off. . . that man
walked in here with his hands over his gut to keep his insides from spilling right out on this desk . . .

ORDERLY

I heard. . . .

NURSE

. . . and that man may live, or he may not live, and the
wagers are heavy that he will not live . . . but we are not
one bit more concerned for that man than we are for
His Honor . . . no sir.

ORDERLY *(Chuckling)*

I like your contempt.

NURSE

You what? You like my *contempt*, do you? Well now, don't misunderstand me. Just what do you think I meant? What have you got it in your mind that I was saying?

ORDERLY

Why, it's a matter of proportion. Surely you don't *condone* the fact that the mayor and his piles, and that poor man lying up there . . . ?

NURSE

Condone! Will you listen to that: condone! My! Aren't you the educated one? What . . . what does that word mean, boy? That word condone? Hunh? You do talk some, don't you? You have a great deal to learn. Now it's true that the poor man lying up there with his guts coming out could be a nigger for all the attention he'd get if His Honor should start shouting for something . . . he could be on the operating table . . . and they'd drop his insides right on the floor and come running if the mayor should want his cigar lit. . . . But that is the way things *are*. Those are facts. You had better acquaint yourself with some realities.

ORDERLY

I know . . . I know the mayor is an important man. He *is* impressive . . . even lying on his belly like he is. . . . I'd like to get to talk to him.

NURSE

Don't you know it! TALK to him! Talk to the mayor? What for?

ORDERLY

I've told you. I've told you I don't intend to stay here carrying crap pans and washing out the operating theatre until I have a . . . a long gray beard . . . I'm . . . I'm going beyond that.

NURSE (*Patronizing*)

Sure.

ORDERLY

I've told you . . . I'm going beyond that. This . . .

NURSE

(*Shakes her head in amused disbelief*) Oh, my. Listen . . . you should count yourself lucky, boy. Just what do you think is going to happen to you? Is His Honor, the mayor, going to rise up out of his sickbed and take a personal interest in you? Write a letter to the President, maybe? And is Mr. Roosevelt going to send his wife, Lady Eleanor, down here after you? Or is it in your plans that you are going to be handed a big fat scholarship somewhere to the north of Johns Hopkins? Boy, you just don't know! I'll tell you something . . . you are lucky as you are. Whatever do you expect?

ORDERLY

What's been promised. . . . Nothing more. Just that.

NURSE

Promised! Promised? Oh, boy, I'll tell you about promises. Don't you know yet that everything is promises . . . and that is all there is to it? Promises . . . nothing more! I am personally sick of promises. Would you like to hear a little poem? Would you like me to recite some verse for you? Here is a little poem: "You kiss the niggers and I'll kiss the Jews and we'll stay in the White House as long as we choose." And that . . . according to what I am told . . . that is what Mr. and Mrs. Roosevelt sit at the breakfast table and sing to each other over their orange

juice, right in the White House. Promises, boy! Promises
. . . and that is what they are going to stay.

NURSE

There are *some* people who believe in more than promises. . . .

ORDERLY

NURSE

Hunh?

ORDERLY *(Cautious now)*

I say, there are some people who believe in more than
promises; there are some people who believe in action.

NURSE

What's that? What did you say?

ORDERLY

Action . . . ac— . . . Never mind.

NURSE *(Her eyes narrow)*

No . . . no, go on now . . . action? What kind of action
do you mean?

ORDERLY

I don't *mean* anything . . . all I said was . . .

NURSE

I heard you. You know . . . I know what you been
doing. You been listening to the great white doctor again
. . . that big, good-looking blond intern you *admire* so
much because he is so liberal-thinking, eh? My suitor?
(Laughs) My suitor . . . my very own white knight, who
is wasting his time patching up decent folk right here
when there is dying going on in Spain. *(Exaggerated)*
Oh, there is dying in Spain. And he is held here! That's
who you have been listening to.

ORDERLY

I don't mean that. . . . I don't pay any attention . . . (*Weakly*) to that kind of talk. I do my job here . . . I try to keep . . .

NURSE (*Contemptuous*)

You try to keep yourself on the good side of everybody, don't you, boy? You stand there and you nod your kinky little head and say yes'm, yes'm, at everything I say, and then when he's here you go off in a corner and you get him and you sympathize with him . . . you get him to tell you about . . . promises! . . . and . . . and . . . action! . . . I'll tell you right now, he's going to get himself into trouble . . . and you're helping him right along.

ORDERLY

No, now. I don't . . .

NURSE (*With some disgust*)

All that talk of his! Action! I know all what he talks about . . . like about that bunch of radicals came through here last spring . . . causing the rioting . . . that arson! Stuff like that. Didn't . . . didn't you have someone get banged up in that?

ORDERLY (*Contained*)

My uncle got run down by a lorry full of state police . . .

NURSE

. . . which the Governor called out because of the rioting . . . and that arson! Action! That was a fine bunch of action. Is that what you mean? Is that what you get him off in a corner and get him to talk about . . . and pretend you're interested? Listen, boy . . . if you're going to get yourself in with those folks, you'd better . . .

ORDERLY (*Quickly*)

I'm not mixed up with any folks . . . honestly . . . I'm not. I just want to . . .

NURSE

I'll tell you what you just want. . . . I'll tell you what you just want if you have any mind to keep this good job you've got. . . . You just shut your ears . . . and you keep that mouth closed tight, too. All this talk about what you are going to go beyond! You keep walking a real tight line here, and . . . and at night . . . (*She begins to giggle*) . . . and at night, if you want to, on your own time . . . at night you keep right on putting that bleach on your hands and your neck and your face . . .

ORDERLY

I do no such thing!

NURSE (*In full laughter*)

. . . and you keep right on bleaching away . . . b-l-e-a-c-h-i-n-g a-w-a-y . . . but you do that on your own time . . . you can do all that on your own time.

ORDERLY (*Pleading*)

I do no such thing!

NURSE

The hell you don't! You are such a . . .

ORDERLY

That kind of talk is very . . .

NURSE

. . . you are so mixed up! You are going to be one funny sight. You, over there in a corner playing up to him . . .

well, boy, you are going to be one funny sight come the millennium. . . . The great black mob marching down the street, banners in the air . . . that great black mob . . . and you right there in the middle, your bleached-out, snowy-white face in the middle of the pack like that . . . (*She breaks down in laughter*) . . . oh . . . oh, my . . . oh. I tell you, that will be quite a sight.

ORDERLY (*Plaintive*)

I wish you'd stop that.

NURSE

Quite a sight.

ORDERLY

I wish you wouldn't make fun of me . . . I don't give you any cause.

NURSE

Oh, my . . . oh, I *am* sorry . . . I am *so* sorry.

ORDERLY

I don't think I give you any cause. . . .

NURSE

You don't, eh?

ORDERLY

No.

NURSE

Well . . . you *are* a true little gentleman, that's for sure . . . you *are* polite . . . and deferential . . . and you are a genuine little ass-licker, if I ever saw one. Tell me, boy . . .

ORDERLY

(*Stiffening a little*) There is no need . . .

NURSE

(*Maliciously solicitous*) Tell me, boy . . . is it true that
you have Uncle Tom'd yourself right out of the bosom of
your family . . . right out of your circle of acquaintances?
Is it true, young man, that you are now an inhabitant of
no-man's-land, on the one side shunned and disowned by
your brethren, and on the other an object of contempt
and derision to your betters? Is that your problem, son?

ORDERLY

You . . . you shouldn't do that. I . . . work hard . . . I
try to advance myself . . . I give nobody trouble.

NURSE

I'll tell you what you do. . . . You go north, boy . . .
you go up to New York City, where nobody's any better
than anybody else . . . get up north, boy. (*Abrupt change
of tone*) But before you do anything like that, you run
on downstairs and get me a pack of cigarettes.

ORDERLY

(*Pauses. Is about to speak; thinks better of it; moves off
to door, rear*) Yes'm.
        (*Exits*)

NURSE

        (*Watches him leave. After he is gone, shakes her
        head, laughs, parodies him*)
Yes'm . . . yes'm . . . ha, ha, ha! You white niggers kill
me.

        (*She picks up her desk phone, dials a number, as
        the lights come up on*)

SCENE FIVE

*Which is both the hospital set of the preceding
scene and, as well, on the raised platform, another
admissions desk of another hospital. The desk is
empty. The phone rings, twice. The* SECOND NURSE
comes in, slowly, filing her nails, maybe.

SECOND NURSE

(*Lazily answering the phone*) Mercy Hospital.

NURSE

Mercy Hospital! Mercy, indeed, you away from your
desk all the time. *Some* hospitals are run better than
others; some nurses stay at their posts.

SECOND NURSE (*Bored*)

Oh, hi. What do you want?

NURSE

I don't *want* anything. . . .

SECOND NURSE

(*Pause*) Oh. Well, what did you call for?

NURSE

I didn't call *for* anything. I (*Shrugs*) just called.

SECOND NURSE

Oh.

(*The lights dim a little on the two nurses.
Music.
Car sounds up*)

JACK'S VOICE

(*Laughs*) I tell you, honey, he didn't like that. No, sir, he didn't. You comfortable, honey. Hunh? You just lean back and enjoy the ride, baby; we're makin' good time. Yes, we are makin' . . . WATCH OUT! WATCH . . .

> (*Sound of crash. . . . Silence*)

Honey . . . baby . . . we have crashed . . . you all right? . . . BESSIE! BESSIE!

> (*Music up again, fading as the lights come up full again on the two nurses*)

NURSE

. . . and, what else? Oh, yeah; *we* have got the mayor here.

SECOND NURSE

That's nice. What's he doin'?

NURSE

He isn't *doin'* anything; he is a patient here.

SECOND NURSE

Oh. Well, *we* had the mayor's wife *here* . . . last April.

NURSE

Unh-hunh. Well, *we* got the mayor *here*, now.

SECOND NURSE (*Very bored*)

Unh-hunh. Well, that's nice.

NURSE

(*Turns, sees the* INTERN *entering*) Oh, lover-boy just walked in; I'll call you later, hunh?

SECOND NURSE

Unh-hunh.

> (*They both hang up. The lights fade on the* SECOND NURSE)

SCENE SIX

NURSE

Well, how is the Great White Doctor this evening?

INTERN (*Irritable*)

Oh ... drop it.

NURSE

Oh, my . . . where is your cheerful demeanor this evening, Doctor?

INTERN

(*Smiling in spite of himself*) How do you do it? How do you manage to just dismiss things from your mind? How can you say a . . . cheerful hello to someone . . . dismissing from your mind . . . excusing yourself for the vile things you have said the evening before?

NURSE (*Lightly*)

I said nothing vile. I put you in your place . . . that's all. I . . . I merely put you in your place . . . as I have done before . . . and as I shall do again.

INTERN

(*Is about to say something; thinks better of it; sighs*) Never mind . . . forget about it . . . Did you *see* the sunset?

NURSE (*Mimicking*)

No, I didn't *see* the sunset. *What* is it doing?

INTERN

(*Amused. Puts it on heavily*) The west is burning . . .
fire has enveloped fully half of the continent . . . the . . .
the fingers of the flame stretch upward to the stars . . .
and . . . and there is a monstrous burning circumference
hanging on the edge of the world.

NURSE *(Laughs)*

Oh, my . . . oh, my.

INTERN *(Serious)*

It's a truly beautiful sight. Go out and have a look.

NURSE *(Coquettish)*

Oh, Doctor, I am chained to my desk of pain, so I must
rely on you. . . . Talk the sunset to me, you . . . you
monstrous burning intern hanging on the edge of my
circumference . . . ha, ha, *ha*.

INTERN

(*Leans toward her*) When?

NURSE

When?

INTERN *(Lightly)*

When . . . when are you going to let me nearer, woman?

NURSE

Oh, my!

INTERN

Here am I . . . here am I tangential, while all the while
I would serve more nobly as a radiant, not outward
from, but reversed, plunging straight to your lovely vortex.

NURSE *(Laughs)*

Oh, la! You must keep your mind off my lovely vortex
. . . you just remain . . . uh . . . tangential.

INTERN *(Mock despair)*

How is a man to fulfill himself? Here I offer you love . . .
consider the word . . . love. . . . Here I offer you my
love, my self . . . my bored bed . . .

NURSE

I note your offer . . . your offer is noted. (*Holds out a
clip board*) Here . . . do you want your reports?

INTERN

No . . . I don't want my reports. Give them here. (*Takes
the clip board*)

NURSE

And while you're here with your hot breath on me, hand
me a cigarette. I sent the nigger down for a pack. I ran
out. (*He gives her a cigarette*) Match?

INTERN

Go light it on the sunset. (*Tosses match to her*) He says
you owe him for three packs.

NURSE

(*Lights her cigarette*) Your bored bed . . . indeed.

INTERN

Ma'am . . . the heart yearns, the body burns . . .

NURSE

And *I* haven't time for *in*terns.

INTERN

. . . the heart yearns, the body burns . . . and I haven't

time . . . Oh, I don't know . . . the things you women can do to art.

(*More intimate, but still light*)

Have you told your father, yet? Have you told your father that I am hopelessly in love with you? Have you told him that at night the sheets of my bed are like a tent, poled center-upward in my love for you?

NURSE (*Wry*)

I'll tell him . . . I'll tell my father just that . . . just what you said . . . and he'll be down here after you for talking to a young lady like that! Really!

INTERN

My God! I forgot myself! A cloistered maiden in whose house trousers are never mentioned . . . in which flies, I am sure, are referred to only as winged bugs. Here I thought I was talking to someone, to a certain young nurse, whose collection of anatomical jokes for all occasions . . .

NURSE (*Giggles*)

Oh, you be still, now. (*Lofty*) Besides, just because I play coarse and flip around here . . . to keep my place with the rest of you . . . don't you think for a minute that I relish this turn to the particular from the general. . . . If you don't mind, we'll just cease this talk.

INTERN (*Half sung*)

I'm always in tumescence for you. You'd never guess the things I . . .

NURSE (*Blush-giggle*)

Now stop that! Really, I mean it!

INTERN

Then marry me, woman. If nothing else, marry me.

NURSE

Don't, now.

INTERN

(*Joking and serious at the same time*) Marry me.

NURSE

(*Matter-of-fact, but not unkindly*) I am sick of this talk.
My poor father may have some funny ideas; he may be
having a pretty hard time reconciling himself to things
as they are. But not me! Forty-six dollars a month! Isn't
that right? Isn't that what you make? Forty-six dollars a
month! Boy, you can't afford even to think about marrying. You can't afford marriage. . . . Best you can afford
is lust. That's the best you can afford.

INTERN (*Scathing*)

Oh . . . gentle woman . . . nineteenth-century lady out of
place in this vulgar time . . . maiden versed in petit point
and murmured talk of the weather . . .

NURSE

Now I mean it . . . you can cut that talk right out.

INTERN

. . . type my great-grandfather fought and died for . . .
forty-six dollars a month and the best I can afford is
lust! Jesus, woman!

NURSE

All right . . . you can quit making fun of me. You can
quit it right this minute.

INTERN

I! Making fun of *you* . . . !

NURSE

I am tired of being toyed with; I am tired of your impractical propositions. Must you dwell on what is not going to happen? Must you ask me, constantly, over and over again, the same question to which you are already aware you will get the same answer? Do you get pleasure from it? What unreasonable form of contentment do you derive from persisting in this?

INTERN *(Lightly)*

Because I love you?

NURSE

Oh, that would help matters along; it really would . . . even if it were *true*. The economic realities would pick up their skirts, whoop, and depart before the lance-high, love-smit knight. My knight, whose real and true interest, if we come right down to it, as indicated in the order of your propositions, is, and always has been, a convenient and uncomplicated bedding down.

INTERN

(Smiling, and with great gallantry) I have offered to marry you.

NURSE

Yeah . . . sure . . . you have offered to marry me. The United States is chuck-full of girls who have heard that great promise—I will marry you . . . I will marry you . . . IF! If! The great promise with its great conditional attached to it. . . .

INTERN *(Amused)*

Who are you pretending to be?

NURSE (*Abrupt*)

What do you mean?

INTERN (*Laughing*)

Oh, *nothing.*

NURSE

(*Regards him silently for a moment; then*) Marry me! Do you know . . . do you know that nigger I sent to fetch me a pack of butts . . . do you know he is in a far better position . . . realistically, economically . . . to ask to marry me than you are? Hunh? Do you know that? That nigger! Do you know that nigger outearns you . . . and by a *lot?*

INTERN

(*Bows to her*) I know he does . . . and I know what value you, you and your famous family, put on such things. So, I have an idea for you . . . why don't you just *ask* that nigger to marry you? 'Cause, boy, he'd never ask you! I'm sure if you told your father about it, it would give him some pause at first, because we know what type of man your father is . . . don't we? . . . But then he would think about it . . . and realize the advantages of the match . . . realistically . . . economically . . . and he would find some way to adjust his values, in consideration of your happiness, and security. . . .

NURSE

(*Flicks her still-lit cigarette at him, hard; hits him with it*) You are disgusting!

INTERN

Damn you, bitch!

NURSE

Disgusting!

INTERN

Realistic . . . practical . . . (*A little softer, now*) Your
family is a famous *name*, but those thousand acres are
gone, and the pillars of your house are blistered and
flaking . . . (*Harder*) Not that your family ever *had*,
within human memory, a thousand acres to go . . . *or*
a house with pillars in the first place. . . .

NURSE *(Angry)*

I am fully aware of what is true and what is not true.
(*Soberly*) Go about your work and leave me be.

INTERN *(Sweetly)*

Aw.

NURSE

I said . . . leave me be.

INTERN

(*Brushing himself*) It is a criminal offense to set fire
to interns . . . orderlies you may burn at will, unless you
have other plans for them . . . but interns . . .

NURSE

. . . are a dime a dozen. (*Giggles*) Did I burn you?

INTERN

No, you did not burn me.

NURSE

That's too bad . . . would have served you right if I had.
(*Pauses; then smiles*) I'm sorry, honey.

INTERN *(Mock formal)*

I accept your apology . . . and I await your surrender.

NURSE *(Laughs)*

Well, you just await it. (*A pause*) Hey, what are you going to do about the mayor being here now?

INTERN

What am I supposed to do about it? I am on emergencies, and he is not an emergency case.

NURSE

I told you . . . I told you what you should do.

INTERN

I know . . . I should go upstairs to his room . . . I should pull up a chair, and I should sit down and I should say, How's tricks, Your Honor?

NURSE

Well, you make fun if you want to . . . but if you listen to me, you'll know you need some people *behind* you.

INTERN

Strangers!

NURSE

Strangers don't say strangers . . . not if you don't let them. He could do something for you if he had a mind to.

INTERN

Yes he could . . . indeed, he *could* do something for me. . . . He could give me his car . . . he could make me a present of his Cord automobile. . . . That would be the finest thing any mayor ever did for a private citizen. Have you seen that car?

NURSE

Have I seen that car? Have I seen this . . . have I seen that? Cord automobiles and . . . and sunsets . . . those are . . . fine preoccupations. Is that what you think about? Huh? Driving a fine car into a fine sunset?

INTERN *(Quietly)*

Lord knows, I'd like to get away from here.

NURSE *(Nodding)*

I know . . . I know. Well, maybe you're going to *have* to get away from here. People are aware how dissatisfied you are . . . people have heard a lot about your . . . dissatisfactions. . . . My father has heard . . . people got wind of the way you feel about things. People here aren't good enough for your attentions. . . . Foreigners . . . a bunch of foreigners who are cutting each other up in their own business . . . that's where you'd like to be, isn't it?

INTERN *(Quietly; intensely)*

There are over half a million people killed in that war! Do you know that? By airplanes. . . . Civilians! You misunderstand me so! I am . . . all right . . . this way. . . . My dissatisfactions . . . you call them that . . . my dissatisfactions have nothing to do with loyalties. . . . I am not concerned with politics . . . but I have a sense of urgency . . . a dislike of waste . . . stagnation . . . I am *stranded* . . . *here*. . . . My talents are not large . . . but the emergencies of the emergency ward of this second-rate hospital in this second-rate state . . . No! . . . it isn't enough. Oh, you listen to me. If I could . . . if I could bandage the arm of one person . . . if I could be over there right this minute . . . you could take the city of Memphis . . . you could take the whole state . . . and don't you forget I was born here . . . you could take the whole goddam state. . . .

NURSE *(Hard)*

Well, I have a very good idea of how we could arrange that. I have a dandy idea. . . . We could just tell the mayor about the way you feel, and he'd be delighted to help you on your way . . . out of this hospital at the very least, and maybe out of the state! And I don't think he'd be giving you any Cord automobile as a going-away present, either. He'd set you out, all right . . . he'd set you right out on your *butt!* That's what he'd do.

INTERN

(With a rueful half-smile) Yes . . . yes . . . I imagine he would. I feel lucky . . . I feel doubly fortunate, now . . . having you . . . feeling the way we do about each other.

NURSE

You are so sarcastic!

INTERN

Well, how the hell do you expect me to behave?

NURSE

Just . . . *(Laughs)* . . . oh, boy, this is good . . . just like I told the nigger . . . you walk a straight line, and you do your job . . . *(Turns coy, here)* . . . and . . . and unless you are kept late by some emergency more pressing than your . . . *(Smiles wryly)* . . . "love" . . . for me . . . I may let you drive me home tonight . . . in your beat-up Chevvy.

INTERN

Woman, as always I anticipate with enormous pleasure the prospect of driving you home . . . a stop along the way . . . fifteen minutes or so of . . . of tantalizing preliminary love play ending in an infuriating and inconclusive wrestling match, during which you hiss of the . . .

the liberties I should not take, and I sound the horn once or twice accidentally with my elbow . . .

(*She giggles at this*)

. . . and, finally, in my beat-up car, in front of your father's beat-up house . . . a kiss of searing intensity . . . a hand in the right place . . . briefly . . . and your hasty departure within. I am looking forward to this ritual . . . as I always do.

NURSE (*Pleased*)

Why, thank you.

INTERN

I look forward to this ritual because of how it sets me apart from other men . . .

NURSE

Aw . . .

INTERN

. . . because I am probably the only white man under sixty in two counties who has *not* had the pleasure of . . .

NURSE

LIAR! You no-account mother-grabbing son of a nigger!

INTERN (*Laughs*)

Boy! Watch you go!

NURSE

FILTH! You are filth!

INTERN

I am honest . . . an honest man. Let me make you an honest woman.

NURSE

(*Steaming . . . her rage between her teeth*) You have
done it, boy . . . you have played around with me and
you have done it. I am going to get you . . . I am going
to fix you . . . I am going to see to it that you are
through here . . . do you understand what I'm telling
you?

INTERN

There is no ambiguity in your talk now, honey.

NURSE

You're damn right there isn't.
>   (*The* ORDERLY *re-enters from stage-rear. The*
>   NURSE *sees him*)

Get out of here!
>   (*But he stands there*)

Do you hear me? You get the hell out of here! GO!
>   (*He retreats, exits, to silence*)

INTERN (*Chuckling*)

King of the castle. My, you *are* something.

NURSE

Did you get what I was telling you?

INTERN

Why, I heard every word . . . every sweet syllable. . . .

NURSE

You have overstepped yourself . . . and you are going to
wish you hadn't. I'll get my father . . . I'll have you
done with *myself.*

INTERN (*Cautious*)

Aw, come on, now.

NURSE

I mean it.

INTERN *(Lying badly)*

Now look . . . you don't think I meant . . .

NURSE *(Mimicking)*

Now you don't think I meant . . . *(Laughs broadly)* Oh,
my . . . you are the funny one.
> *(Her threat, now, has no fury, but is filled with
> quiet conviction)*

I said I'll fix you . . . and I will. You just go along with
your work . . . you do your job . . . but what I said
. . . you keep that burning in the back of your brain.
We'll go right along, you and I, and we'll be civil . . .
and it'll be as though nothing had happened . . . nothing
at all. *(Laughs again)* Honey, your neck is in the *noose*
. . . and I have a whip . . . and I'll set the horse from
under you . . . when it pleases me.

INTERN *(Wryly)*

It's going to be nice around here.

NURSE

Oh, yes it is. I'm going to enjoy it . . . I really am.

INTERN

Well . . . I'll forget about driving you home tonight. . . .

NURSE

Oh, no . . . you will *not* forget about driving me home
tonight. You will drive me home *tonight* . . . you will
drive me home *tonight* . . . and *tomorrow* night . . .
you will see me to my *door* . . . you will be my gallant.
We will have things between us a little bit the way I am
told things *used* to be. You will *court* me, boy, and you
will do it *right!*

INTERN

(*Stares at her for a moment*) You impress me. No matter what else, I've got to admit that.

> (*The* NURSE *laughs wildly at this.*
> *Music.*
> *The lights on this hospital set fade, and come up on the* SECOND NURSE, *at her desk, for*)

SCENE SEVEN

JACK

(*Rushing in*) Ma'am, I need help, quick!

SECOND NURSE

What d'you want here?

JACK

There has been an accident, ma'am . . . I got an injured woman outside in my car. . . .

SECOND NURSE

Yeah? Is that so? Well, you sit down and wait. . . . You go over there and sit down and wait a while.

JACK

This is an emergency! There has been an accident!

SECOND NURSE

YOU WAIT! You just sit down and wait!

JACK

This woman is badly hurt. . . .

SECOND NURSE

YOU COOL YOUR HEELS!

JACK

Ma'am . . . I got Bessie Smith out in that car there. . . .

SECOND NURSE

I DON'T CARE WHO YOU GOT OUT THERE, NIGGER. YOU COOL YOUR HEELS!
> (*Music up.*
> *The lights fade on this scene, come up again on the main hospital scene, on the* NURSE *and the* INTERN, *for*)

SCENE EIGHT

(*Music fades*)

NURSE (*Loud*)

Hey, nigger . . . nigger!
> (*The* ORDERLY *re-enters*)
Give me my cigarettes.

INTERN

I think I'll . . .

NURSE

You stay here!
> (*The* ORDERLY *hands the nurse the cigarettes, cautious and attentive to see what is wrong*)
A person could die for a smoke, the time you take. What'd you do . . . sit downstairs in the can and rest your small, shapely feet . . . hunh?

ORDERLY

You told me to . . . go back outside . . .

NURSE

Before that! What'd you do . . . go to the cigarette *factory?* Did you take a quick run up to Winston-Salem for these?

ORDERLY

No . . . I . . .

NURSE

Skip it. (*To the* INTERN) Where? Where were you planning to go?

INTERN (*Too formal*)

I beg your pardon?

NURSE

I said . . . where did you want to go to? Were you off for coffee?

INTERN

Is that what you want? Now that you have your cigarettes, have you hit upon the idea of having coffee, too? Now that he is back from one errand, are you planning to send me on another?

NURSE (*Smiling wickedly*)

Yeah . . . I think I'd like that . . . keep both of you jumping. I *would* like coffee, and I *would* like you to get it for me. So why don't you just trot right across the hall and get me some? And I like it good and hot . . . and strong . . .

INTERN

. . . and black . . . ?

NURSE

Cream! . . . and sweet . . . and in a hurry!

INTERN

I guess your wish is my command . . . hunh?

NURSE

You bet it is!

INTERN

(*Moves halfway to the door, stage-rear, then pauses*)

I just had a lovely thought . . . that maybe sometime when you are sitting there at your desk opening mail with that stiletto you use for a letter opener, you might slip and tear open your arm . . . then you could come running into the emergency . . . and I could be there when you came running in, blood coming out of you like water out of a faucet . . . and I could take ahold of your arm . . . and just hold it . . . just hold it . . . and watch it flow . . . just hold on to you and watch your blood flow. . . .

NURSE

(*Grabs up the letter opener . . . holds it up*)

This? More likely between your ribs!

INTERN (*Exiting*)

One coffee, lady.

NURSE

(*After a moment of silence, throws the letter opener back down on her desk*)

I'll take care of him. CRACK! I'll crack that whip. (*To the* ORDERLY) What are you standing there for . . . hunh? You like to watch what's going on?

ORDERLY

I'm no voyeur.

NURSE

You what? You like to listen in? You take pleasure in it?

ORDERLY

I said no.

NURSE *(Half to herself)*

I'll bet you don't. I'll take care of him . . . talking to me like that . . . I'll crack that whip. Let him just wait.
(*To the* ORDERLY, *now*)
My father says that Francisco Franco is going to be victorious in that war over there . . . that he's going to win . . . and that it's just wonderful.

ORDERLY

He does?

NURSE

Yes, he does. My father says that Francisco Franco has got them licked, and that they're a bunch of radicals, anyway, and it's all to the good . . . just wonderful.

ORDERLY

Is that so?

NURSE

I've told you my father is a . . . a historian, so he isn't just anybody. His opinion counts for something special. It *still* counts for something special. He says anybody wants to go over there and get mixed up in that thing has got it coming to him . . . whatever happens.

ORDERLY

I'm sure your father is an informed man, and . . .

NURSE

What?

ORDERLY

I said . . . I said . . . I'm sure your father is an informed man, and . . . his opinion is to be respected.

NURSE

That's right, boy . . . you just jump to it and say what you think people want to hear . . . you be both sides of the coin. Did you . . . did you hear him threaten me there? Did you?

ORDERLY

Oh, now . . . I don't think . . .

NURSE *(Steely)*

You heard him threaten me!

ORDERLY

I don't think . . .

NURSE

For such a smart boy . . . you are so dumb. I don't know what I am going to do with you.
    (*She is thinking of the* INTERN *now, and her ex-pression shows it*)
You refuse to comprehend things, and that bodes badly . . . it does. Especially considering it is all but arranged . . .

ORDERLY

What is all but arranged?

NURSE

    (*A great laugh, but mirthless. She is barely under control*)
Why, don't you know, boy? Didn't you know that you and I are practically engaged?

ORDERLY

I . . . I don't . . .

NURSE

Don't you know about the economic realities? Haven't you been appraised of the way things *are*? (*She giggles*) Our knights are gone forth into sunsets . . . behind the wheels of Cord cars . . . the acres have diminished and the paint is flaking . . . that there is a great . . . *abandonment?*

ORDERLY (*Cautious*)

I don't understand you. . . .

NURSE

No kidding? (*Her voice shakes*) No kidding . . . you don't understand me? Why? What's the matter, boy, don't you get the idea?

ORDERLY (*Contained, but angry*)

I think you'd tire of riding me some day. I think you *would*. . . .

NURSE

You go up to Room 206, right now . . . you go up and tell the mayor that when his butt's better we have a marrying job for him.

ORDERLY (*With some distaste*)

Really . . . you go much too far. . . .

NURSE

Oh, I do, do I? Well, let me tell you something . . . I am sick of it! I am *sick*. I am sick of everything in this hot, stupid, fly-ridden *world*. I am sick of the disparity between things as they are, and as they should be! I am sick of this desk . . . this uniform . . . it scratches. . . . I am sick of the sight of *you* . . . the *thought* of you makes me . . . *itch*. . . . I am sick of him. (*Soft now: a chant*) I am sick of talking to people on the phone in this damn stupid hospital. . . . I am sick of the smell of Lysol . . . I could die of it. . . . I am sick of going to bed and I am sick of waking up. . . . I am tired . . . I am tired of the truth . . . and I am tired of lying about the truth . . . I am tired of my skin. . . . I WANT OUT!

ORDERLY

(*After a short pause*) Why don't you go into emergency . . . and lie down?
            (*He approaches her*)

NURSE

Keep away from me.
            (*At this moment the outside door bursts open and* JACK *plunges into the room. He is all these things: drunk, shocked, frightened. His face should be cut, but no longer bleeding. His clothes should be dirtied . . . and in some disarray. He pauses, a few steps into the room, breathing hard*)

NURSE

Whoa! Hold on there, you.

ORDERLY (*Not advancing*)

What do you want?

JACK

(*After more hard breathing; confused*) What . . . ?

NURSE

You come banging in through that door like that? What's the matter with you? (*To the* ORDERLY) Go see what's the matter with him.

ORDERLY (*Advancing slightly*)

What do you *want?*

JACK (*Very confused*)

What do I want . . . ?

ORDERLY (*Backing off*)

You can't come in here like this . . . banging your way
in here . . . don't you know any better?

NURSE

You drunk?

JACK

(*Taken aback by the irrelevance*) I've been drinking . . .
yes . . . all right . . . I'm drunk. (*Intense*) I got someone outside . . .

NURSE

You stop that yelling. This is a white hospital, you.

ORDERLY (*Nearer the* NURSE)

That's right. She's right. This is a private hospital . . . a
semiprivate hospital. If you go on . . . into the city . . .

JACK (*Shakes his head*)

No. . . .

NURSE

Now you listen to me, and you get this straight . . .
(*Pauses just perceptibly, then says the word, but with
no special emphasis*) . . . nigger . . . this is a semiprivate
white hospital . . .

JACK (*Defiant*)

I don't care!

NURSE

Well, you *get* on. . . .

ORDERLY
(*As the* INTERN *re-enters with two containers of
     coffee*)
You go on now . . . you go . . .

INTERN

What's all this about?

ORDERLY

I told him to go on into Memphis . . .

INTERN

Be quiet. (*To* JACK) What is all this about?

JACK

Please . . . I got a woman . . .

NURSE

You been told to move on.

INTERN

You got a woman . . .

JACK

Outside . . . in the car. . . . There was an accident . . .
there is blood. . . . Her arm . . .

INTERN
(*After thinking for a moment, looking at the*
     NURSE, *moves toward the outside door*)
All right . . . we'll go see. (*To the* ORDERLY, *who hangs
back*) Come on, you . . . let's go.

ORDERLY

(*Looks to the* NURSE) We told him to go on into Memphis.

NURSE

(*To the* INTERN, *her eyes narrowing*) Don't you go out there!

INTERN

(*Ignoring her; to the* ORDERLY) You heard me . . . come on!

NURSE (*Strong*)

I told you . . . DON'T GO OUT THERE!

INTERN (*Softly, sadly*)

Honey . . . you going to fix me? You going to have the mayor throw me out of here on my butt? Or are you going to arrange it in Washington to have me *deported?* What *are* you going to do . . . hunh?

NURSE (*Between her teeth*)

Don't go out there. . . .

INTERN

Well, honey, whatever it is you're going to do . . . it might as well be now as any other time.
        (*He and the* ORDERLY *move to the outside door*)

NURSE

        (*Half angry, half plaintive, as they exit*)
Don't go!
        (*After they exit*)
I warn you! I *will* fix you. You go out that door . . . you're through here.
        (JACK *moves to a vacant area near the bench, stage-right. The* NURSE *lights a cigarette*)

I told you I'd fix you . . . I'll fix you. (*Now, to* JACK)
I think I said this was a white hospital.

JACK (*Wearily*)

I know, lady . . . you told me.

NURSE

(*Her attention on the door*) You don't have sense enough
to do what you're told . . . you make trouble for yourself . . . you make trouble for other people.

JACK (*Sighing*)

I don't care. . . .

NURSE

You'll care!

JACK

(*Softly, shaking his head*) No . . . I won't care. (*Now,
half to her, half to himself*) We were driving along . . .
not very fast . . . I don't think we were driving fast . . .
we were in a hurry, yes . . . and I had been drinking
. . . *we* had been drinking . . . but I *don't* think we were
driving fast . . . not too fast . . .

NURSE

(*Her speeches now are soft comments on his*)
. . . driving drunk on the road . . . it not even dark
yet . . .

JACK

. . . but then there was a car . . . I hadn't seen it . . . it
couldn't have seen me . . . from a side road . . . hard,
fast, sudden . . . (*Stiffens*) . . . *CRASH!* (*Loosens*)
. . . and we weren't thrown . . . both of us . . . both
cars stayed on the road . . . but we were stopped . . .
my motor, running. . . . I turned it off . . . the door

. . . the right door was all smashed in. . . . That's all it was . . . no more damage than that . . . but we had been riding along . . . laughing . . . it was cool driving, but it was warm out . . . and she had her arm out the window . . .

NURSE

. . . serves you right . . . drinking on the road . . .

JACK

. . . and I said . . . I said, Honey, we have crashed . . . you all right? (*His face contorts*) And I looked . . . and the door was all pushed in . . . she was caught there . . . where the door had pushed in . . . her right side, crushed into the torn door, the door crushed into her right side. . . . BESSIE! BESSIE! . . . (*More to the* NURSE, *now*) . . . but ma'am . . . her arm . . . her right arm . . . was torn off . . . almost torn off from her shoulder . . . and there was blood . . . SHE WAS BLEEDING SO . . . !

NURSE (*From a distance*)

Like water from a faucet . . . ? Oh, that is terrible . . . terrible. . . .

JACK

I didn't wait for nothin' . . . the other people . . . the other car . . . I started up . . . I started . . .

NURSE (*More alert*)

You took *off?* . . . You took off from an accident?

JACK

Her arm, ma'am . . .

NURSE

You probably got police looking for you right now . . . you know that?

JACK

Yes, ma'am . . . I suppose so . . . and I drove . . . there
was a hospital about a mile up . . .

NURSE

(*Snapping to attention*) THERE! You went somewhere
else? You been somewhere else already? What are you
doing *here* with that woman then, hunh?

JACK

At the hospital . . . I came in to the desk and I told them
what had happened . . . and they said, you sit down and
wait . . . you go over there and sit down and wait a while.
WAIT! It was a white hospital, ma'am . . .

NURSE

This is a white hospital, too.

JACK

I said . . . this is an emergency . . . there has been an
accident. . . . YOU WAIT! You just sit down and wait.
. . . I told them . . . I told them it was an emergency
. . . I said . . . this woman is badly hurt. . . . YOU
COOL YOUR HEELS! . . . I said, Ma'am, I got Bessie
Smith out in that car there. . . . I DON'T CARE WHO
YOU GOT OUT THERE, NIGGER . . . YOU COOL
YOUR HEELS! . . . I couldn't wait there . . . her in
the car . . . so I left there . . . I drove on . . . I stopped
on the road and I was told where to come . . . and I
came here.

NURSE (*Numb, distant*)

I know who she is . . . I heard her sing. (*Abruptly*)
You give me your name! You can't take off from an accident like that . . . I'll phone the police; I'll tell them
where you are!

(*The* INTERN *and the* ORDERLY *re-enter. Their uniforms are bloodied. The* ORDERLY *moves stage-rear, avoiding* JACK. *The* INTERN *moves in, staring at* JACK)

NURSE

He drove away from an accident . . . he just took off . . . and he didn't come right here, either . . . he's been to one hospital *already*. I *warned* you not to get mixed up in this. . . .

INTERN *(Softly)*

Shut up!
(*Moves toward* JACK, *stops in front of him*)
You tell me something . . .

NURSE

I warned you! You didn't listen to me . . .

JACK

You want my name, too . . . is that what you want?

INTERN

No, that's not what I want.
(*He is contained, but there is a violent emotion inside him*)
You tell me something. When you brought her here . . .

JACK

I brought her here. . . . They wouldn't help her. . . .

INTERN

All right. When you brought her here . . . when you brought this woman *here* . . .

NURSE

Oh, this is no plain woman . . . this is no ordinary nigger . . . this is Bessie Smith!

INTERN

When you brought this woman *here* . . . when you drove
up *here* . . . when you brought this woman *here* . . .
DID YOU KNOW SHE WAS DEAD?
> (*Pause*)

NURSE

Dead! . . . This nigger brought a dead woman here?

INTERN

(*Afraid of the answer*) Well . . . ?

NURSE (*Distantly*)

Dead . . . dead.

JACK

(*Wearily; turning, moving toward the outside door*) Yes
. . . I knew she was dead. She died on the way here.

NURSE

(*Snapping to*) Where you going? Where do you think
you're going? I'm going to get the police here for you!

JACK

> (*At the door*)

Just outside.

INTERN

> (*As* JACK *exits*)

WHAT DID YOU EXPECT *ME* TO DO, EH? WHAT
WAS *I* SUPPOSED TO *DO*?
> (JACK *pauses for a moment, looks at him
> blankly, closes the door behind him*)

TELL ME! WHAT WAS I SUPPOSED TO DO?

NURSE (*Slyly*)

Maybe . . . maybe he thought you'd bring her back to

life . . . great white doctor. (*Her laughter begins now, mounts to hysteria*) Great . . . white . . . doctor. . . . Where are you going to go now . . . great . . . white . . . doctor? You are finished. You have had your last patient here. . . . Off you go, boy! You have had your last patient . . . a nigger . . . a dead nigger lady . . . WHO SINGS. Well . . . I sing, too, boy . . . I sing real good. You want to hear me sing? Hunh? You want to hear the way I sing? HUNH?

> (*Here she begins to sing and laugh at the same time. The singing is tuneless, almost keening, and the laughter is almost crying*)

INTERN

> (*Moves to her*)

Stop that! Stop that!

> (*But she can't. Finally he slaps her hard across the face. Silence. She is frozen, with her hand to her face where he hit her. He backs toward the rear door*)

ORDERLY

> (*His back to the wall*)

I never heard of such a thing . . . bringing a dead woman here like that. . . . I don't know what people can be thinking of sometimes. . . .

> (*The* INTERN *exits. The room fades into silhouette again. . . . The great sunset blazes; music up*)

CURTAIN

Fam and Yam

AN IMAGINARY INTERVIEW
(1960)

FIRST PERFORMANCE: August 27, 1960. Westport, Conn.

The White Barn

Fam and Yam

The Players:

The Famous American Playwright (hereafter called FAM)—a no-longer thin gentleman, a year or so either side of fifty. What does he look like most? . . . a slightly rumpled account executive? . . . a faintly foppish Professor of History? Either one will do.

The Young American Playwright (hereafter called YAM)—an intense, bony young man, whose crew cut is in need of a trim; sweat socks, an overlong scarf, an old issue of *Evergeen Review* under one arm.

The Scene:

The living room of the East Side apartment of a famous American playwright; a view of the bridge, white walls; a plum-colored sofa, two Modiglianis, one Braque, a Motherwell and a Kline.

A Sunday afternoon.

At the beginning, FAM is alone, reading, on the plum-colored sofa, a decanter before him, a glass of sherry beside him. The door chime chimes, from the entrance hall, off-stage, L. FAM looks up, consults his wrist watch, frowns, puts down his book, drinks off his sherry, rises, moves off as the door chime chimes again. Maybe he clears his throat as he moves off. Sound of voices whence FAM vanished. . . . "Well, now, how do you do, sir." FAM re-enters, followed by YAM.

FAM

(*Consulting his wrist watch again*) Well, sir. Come in, come in.

YAM

(*Bounding behind him*) I'm early; I apologize.

FAM

Are you? (*Consults his wrist watch again*) Well, so you are. It doesn't matter, though. (*Indicating a chair beside the plum-colored sofa*) Won't you . . . ?

YAM

(*With a quick glance at the paintings*) Ah!

FAM

Hm?

YAM

It must be wonderful to throw away the reproductions!

FAM

The what?

YAM

Your paintings . . . it must be wonderful to throw away the . . .

FAM

Oh . . . yes. (*Indicating the chair again*) Won't you . . . ?

YAM

Very nice place!

FAM

Uh . . . thank you. (*Indicating the chair again*) Shall we . . . ?

YAM

I appreciate your seeing me; I really do.

FAM

Not at all; I was very happy. . . .

YAM

I hesitated writing you; I wasn't sure that . . . well, you know . . . I wasn't sure that I should; perhaps I shouldn't have.

FAM

(*Pause*) Hm? . . . Oh! No, no; I was . . . uh . . . very pleased. (*Moves toward the plum-colored sofa*) Perhaps if we . . .

YAM

(*At the window now*) AH! And this?

FAM

(*Apprehensive*) What?

YAM

This view!

FAM

(*Defensive*) What . . . what about it?

YAM

Joan Crawford, Susan Hayward . . . everybody . . . !

FAM

(*Frightened*) What?

YAM

(*Laughs*) Oh, you know; all those movies they made

. . . and they all had apartments over here, and they always had a view . . . just like this.

FAM

(*Pause*) Um hum. I . . . uh . . . I have your letter here and (*looks around for the letter*) . . . I must say, it was most generous of you to . . .

YAM

(*As* FAM *discovers the letter in his pocket*) Generous! No; not at all. It was the truth.

FAM

(*Smiling modestly; glancing at the letter*) Oh, well, now . . . I . . . it does seem to me . . .

YAM

(*Moving in*) No, it was the truth. You . . . along with a few others . . . Miller, Williams . . . Thornton Wilder, and . . . uh . . . (*Shrugs*) . . . Inge . . . uh . . . you're . . . well, you're right up there.

FAM

(*Without much enthusiasm*) You're very kind.

YAM

I think it's the continuum, really; that's so important.

FAM

The . . . uh . . . ?

YAM

The way you keep writing them . . . one after the other!

FAM

(*Smiling weakly; moving toward the sherry*) Well, it's easier than writing them all at once. Ha, ha, ha.

YAM

(*Rushing on*) I guess what I mean is: You're a real pro.

FAM

(*Considers it; then, proudly*) Yes . . . Yes . . . I suppose you could say that.

YAM

Pro *is* the right word. What's-his-name . . . up at Columbia . . . you know who I mean . . . says that in his book *pro* is synonymous with high-class hack . . . but I don't agree with him there.

FAM

(*Offering the decanter*) Drink?

YAM

No, thanks; I don't drink. . . .

FAM

(*Pouring himself another sherry*) I do.

YAM

. . . this early. I suppose what what's-his-name really means is, that continued popular acceptance of a man's work, like yours. . . .

FAM

(*Too loud*) What did you want to see me about . . . exactly? I couldn't quite tell from your letter . . . I mean, it was a very pleasant letter . . . very flattering . . . but, I'm still not clear. . . .

YAM

. . . but after all, you and a man like that just don't talk the same language.

FAM

(*Puzzled*) Hm? . . . What? . . . Who?

YAM

What's-his-name . . . up at Columbia.

FAM

I . . .

YAM

What I came to see you about . . . maybe I didn't put it too well in my letter . . . is . . . well, I need your advice.

FAM

(*Softly, with becoming modesty.*) Well, I'd be happy . . . I don't know that I'm . . .

YAM

(*Plunging on*) You see . . . I have to do an article on the theatre, and . . .

FAM

(*The corners of his mouth turning upward*) You *have* to?

YAM

Well, I'm not *compelled* to . . . and it *is* on speculation. . . .

FAM

Ah, an *indefinite* article. . . . (*Chuckles.*)

YAM

And . . . uh . . . what? Oh! Yes . . . very good; very good, indeed.

FAM

(*Still chuckling*) Words; words . . . they're such a pleasure.

YAM

At any rate, I *do* have to write this article. . . .

FAM

(*Businesslike . . . for fear of having offended*) Yes; yes, by all means.

YAM

And I *would* appreciate your advice.

FAM

(*Knitting his brow*) Certainly. (*Brightly*) Oh, I've . . . I forgot to congratulate you on your . . . success . . . your . . . uh . . . off-Broadway play.

YAM

(*Pleased*) Oh. . . .

FAM

Yes; yes, indeed . . . you must be very proud. It's called . . . uh . . .

YAM

DILEMMA, DERELICTION AND DEATH.

FAM

Uh . . . yes . . . yes, that's right . . . DILEMMA . . . DEATH. . . .

YAM

DILEMMA, DERELICTION AND DEATH.

FAM

Ah, yes . . . that's it. That's . . . that's quite a mouth-
ful. It's down at the . . . uh . . .

YAM

East Third Street Playhouse.

FAM

Yes; yes. (*Pause*) I must confess I haven't had a chance
to . . . get down there yet. . . .

YAM

Oh, well, I . . .

FAM

Just opened, didn't it? And such good press!

YAM

Four months ago; yes.

FAM

Oh, my . . . that long! (*Pause*) Well, time does . . .
four months already . . . indeed!

YAM

(*Smiling eagerly*) Yes!

FAM

(*Shooting his cuffs, aggressively cheerful*) The new gen-
eration's knocking at the door. Gelber, Richardson, Kopit
. . . (*Shrugs*) . . . Albee . . . you. . . . (*Mock woe*)
You youngsters are going to push us out of the way. . . .

YAM

(*An unintentionally teeth-baring smile*) Well, maybe
there'll be room for all of us.

FAM

(*Rocking back*) Uh . . . well . . . yes! (*Suspiciously*) Let's hope so!

YAM

(*As* FAM *pours himself another sherry*) Well, now . . . about the article.

FAM

(*Apprehensive*) Ah . . . yes . . . that.

YAM

(*Moving in*) It seemed to me best to start right off with a *bang!* (*Strikes a fist into the palm of the other hand.* FAM *jumps slightly*) No pussy-footing around!

FAM

(*Backing off a little.*) No . . . yes; by all means.

YAM

A real attack . . . lay 'em all out . . . put it right on the line . . . and let 'em have it!

FAM

(*Eyeing* YAM) Yes . . . well, we *do* need . . . uh . . . constructive critical journalism (*As his voice trails off*) . . . if there is any such . . .

YAM

(*Breaking in*) What I thought I'd do first . . . is make a list of villains . . . right at the beginning. You see, I'm going to call the piece "In Search of a Hero."

FAM

Well, I think that's . . .

YAM

Dandy, hunh? (*Chuckles . . . goes on*) And so, I thought

I'd make a list . . . right at the top. And list everybody!

FAM

Everybody?

YAM

Everybody! (*Plunging*) And that's where you come in.

FAM

(*Looking toward the hall*) I? . . . I'm not sure I . . .
That's where I need your help. You know these people
. . . you've run up against them . . . you've . . . you've
been exposed to the stupidity . . . the arrogance . . . the
opportunism . . . the . . .

FAM

Well, I suppose I . . .

YAM

I know you have . . . I'm sure of it. Nobody could have
gotten to the position you're in *without* coming in contact
with it.

FAM

(*Cautiously, as he pours himself another sherry*) Well,
now . . . I've had a pretty easy time of it . . . I . . .

YAM

But you *have* run into it!

FAM

(*Wishing himself, or Yam elsewhere*) I *suppose* so . . .
I . . .

YAM

Of course you have! So! Here's the list of villains. (*Paces.
Counts on his fingers*) The theatre owners . . . the pro-

ducers . . . the backers . . . the theatre parties . . . the
unions . . . the critics . . . the directors . . . and the
playwrights themselves. . . . That's the list. (*Smiles*)

FAM

(*Overwhelmed*) That . . . that doesn't . . . (*A weak
smile*) that doesn't leave much room for a hero, does it?

YAM

(*Jumping on it*) That's just the point! Everybody's cul-
pable.

FAM

Oh, my.

YAM

I hope you'll talk frankly.

FAM

Well . . . certainly. . . .

YAM

Because, I don't want to go off half-cocked. . . .

FAM

(*Moving toward the sherry decanter again*) Well, I'm
sure none of us does. Are you sure you don't . . . you
wouldn't like a drink?

YAM

No . . . no, thank you. But you . . . you keep right
on.

FAM

(*Pauses . . . irritated*) Thank you . . . I will.

YAM

(*Ignoring Fam's tone*) Now, for the theatre owners. . . .
I thought one might call them something like . . . igno-
rant, greedy, hit-happy real estate owners.

FAM

(*Shocked . . . amused*) Oh . . . oh, my . . . that is
strong, isn't it?

YAM

And then, the producers. . . . How about: opportunistic,
out-for-a-buck businessmen, masquerading as . . .

FAM

Oh, yes . . . wonderful . . . wonderful . . . very strong.
Oh my!

YAM

You get the idea?

FAM

(*Pouring himself another sherry. He is pacing, now, the
decanter in one hand, the glass in the other*) Yes . . .
yes, I do. That's . . . that's really laying it on the line.
(*Chuckles*)

YAM

And I thought it would be good to say that most of our
playwrights are nothing better than businessmen themselves . . . you know . . . out for the loot . . . just as
cynically as anyone else. . . .

FAM

(*A little tipsy by now*) Oh, ho ho ho ho!

YAM

. . . and that our directors are slick, sleight-of-hand

artists . . . talking all noble and uncompromising *until* they get into rehearsal . . . and *then* . . .

FAM

(*Doubled over with mirth*) Yes . . . yes! Ha ha ha ha!

YAM

. . . and about the critics . . . how they've set themselves up as sociological arbiters . . . misusing their function . . . and . . .

FAM

(*Wildly amused . . . encouraging*) Yes . . . yes . . . go on . . . go on!

YAM

. . . and then tacking into the agencies . . . call them assembly lines or something . . .

FAM

Ha ha ha ha!

YAM

. . . and then the pin-heads . . .

FAM

(*Beside himself*) The pin-heads! Hee hee hee . . . who are they?

YAM

(*Modestly*) Oh, the theatre parties. . . .

FAM

The theatre parties. (*Laughs uncontrollably . . . knocks over an occasional table*) Boy! Give it to 'em, eh? . . . Lay it right on the line! . . . Let 'em all have it! . . . Ha ha ha ha. . . . Mow 'em down!

YAM

(*Beaming*) You like it? You like the idea!

FAM

Like it! I love it! Hee hee hee hee! It's the funniest thing
I've ever heard!

YAM

(*Very serious*) I'm glad.

FAM

C'mon . . . have a drink. Heh heh heh.

YAM

No . . . no . . . I must go. . . . I've taken up too much of
your time already.

FAM

OH, no . . . it's early. C'mon . . . stick around. Ha ha
ha ha.

YAM

(*Extending his hand, which is not taken,* FAM's *hands
being full*) No . . . no, really, sir . . . I must go. Thank
you very much . . . very much indeed.

FAM

Ho ho ho . . . don't mention it. Oh, my . . . I haven't
laughed so much. . . . (*They both move into the entrance
hall. From there . . . goodbyes—thank you's . . . don't
mention its. Sound of door closing.* FAM *re-enters, walks
about pours himself another sherry*) Ha ha ha ha. The
pin-heads! Hee hee hee hee! Oh, my . . . oh my. (*Shakes
his head . . . puts the decanter and glass down, moves to
right the fallen table . . . does so*) The pin-heads! Ha
ha ha ha! (*Roams around the room, giggling, laughing.*

The telephone rings. He moves to it.) Heh heh heh.
Hello . . . ?

YAM'S VOICE

(*Loud—over a speaker*) Uh . . . hello there . . . it's
me again.

FAM

Oh . . . you. . . . C'mon back up an' have a drink.

YAM'S VOICE

Oh no . . . no. . . . I just wanted to thank you again.
I'm just downstairs . . . and I wanted to thank you
again.

FAM

Don't mention it, my boy! Thank *you*. Ha ha ha ha!

YAM'S VOICE

Thank you very much for the interview. Thank you sir.

FAM

You're welcome . . . you're welcome . . . heh heh heh.
(*He hangs up . . . strolls*) You're welcome . . . you're
welcome. (*Suddenly stops*) THE INTERVIEW!!! THE
INTERVIEW!!!!! (*His face turns ashen . . . his mouth
drops open. One of the Modiglianis frowns . . . the
Braque peels . . . the Kline tilts . . . and the Motherwell
crashes to the floor*)

CURTAIN